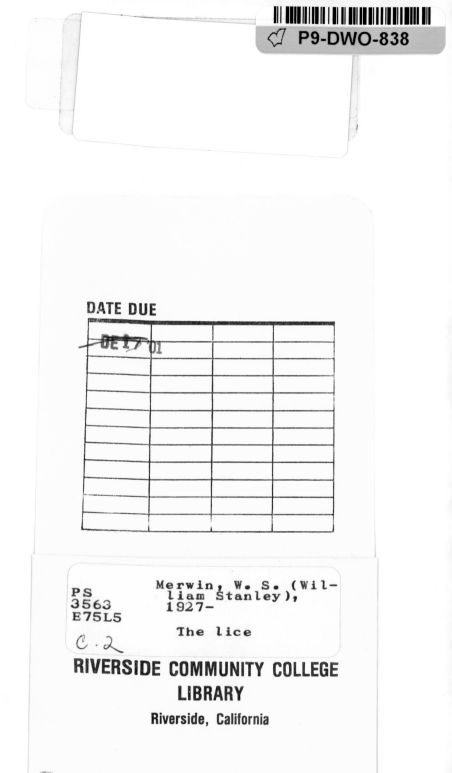

BOOKS BY W. S. MERWIN

POEMS

PROSE

TRANSLATIONS

THE LICE

All men are deceived by the appearances of things, even Homer himself, who was the wisest man in Greece; for he was deceived by boys catching lice: they said to him, "What we have caught and what we have killed we have left behind, but what has escaped us we bring with us."

HERACLITUS

THE LICE

POEMS BY

W. S. MERWIN

ATHENEUM

New York

1 9 8 4

tlantic Monthly;
The Nation;
(THE WAVE,
)NE MASON,
G FOR
YOU ARE, THE
, THE LAST ONE,
IT IS MARCH, BREAD AT MIDNIGHT, PIECES FOR OTHER LIVES,
WHENEVER I GO THERE, THE GODS, APRIL, LOOKING EAST AT
NIGHT, THE DREAM AGAIN, HOW WE ARE SPARED, THE DRAGONFLY,
PROVISION, DIVINITIES, DEATH OF A FAVORITE BIRD); *Princeton
Library Chronicle; The Saturday Evening Post; The Southern
Review; The Sydney Bulletin.*

I would like to thank the Chapelbrook Foundation for a grant
for writing poetry, which has been a great help to me.

FOR GEORGE KIRSTEIN

CONTENTS

THE LICE

THE ANIMALS

All these years behind windows
With blind crosses sweeping the tables

And myself tracking over empty ground
Animals I never saw

I with no voice

Remembering names to invent for them
Will any come back will one

Saying yes

Saying look carefully yes
We will meet again

IS THAT WHAT YOU ARE

New ghost is that what you are
Standing on the stairs of water

No longer surprised

Hope and grief are still our wings
Why we cannot fly

What failure still keeps you
Among us the unfinished

The wheels go on praying

We are not hearing something different
We beat our wings
Why are you there

I did not think I had anything else to give

The wheels say it after me

There are feathers in the ice
We lay the cold across our knees

Today the sun is farther than we think

And at the windows in the knives
You are watching

THE HYDRA

No no the dead have no brothers

The Hydra calls me but I am used to it
It calls me Everybody
But I know my name and do not answer

And you the dead
You know your names as I do not
But at moments you have just finished speaking

The snow stirs in its wrappings
Every season comes from a new place

Like your voice with its resemblances

A long time ago the lightning was practising
Something I thought was easy

I was young and the dead were in other
Ages
As the grass had its own language

Now I forget where the difference falls

One thing about the living sometimes a piece of us
Can stop dying for a moment
But you the dead

Once you go into those names you go on you never
Hesitate
You go on

SOME LAST QUESTIONS

What is the head
             A. Ash
What are the eyes
             A. The wells have fallen in and have
                Inhabitants
What are the feet
             A. Thumbs left after the auction
No what are the feet
             A. Under them the impossible road is moving
                Down which the broken necked mice push
                Balls of blood with their noses
What is the tongue
             A. The black coat that fell off the wall
                With sleeves trying to say something
What are the hands
             A. Paid
No what are the hands
             A. Climbing back down the museum wall
                To their ancestors the extinct shrews that will
                Have left a message
What is the silence
             A. As though it had a right to more
Who are the compatriots
             A. They make the stars of bone

AN END IN SPRING

It is carried beyond itself a little way
And covered with a sky of old bedding

The compatriots stupid as their tables
Go on eating their packages
Selling gloves to the clocks
Doing alright

Ceasing to exist it becomes a deity

It is with the others that are not there
The centuries are named for them the names
Do not come down to us

On the way to them the words
Die

I LIVE UP HERE

I live up here
And a little bit to the left
And I go down only

For the accidents and then
Never a moment too soon

Just the same it's a life it's plenty

The stairs the petals she loves me
Every time
Nothing has changed

Oh down there down there
Every time
The glass knights lie by their gloves of blood

In the pans of the scales the helmets
Brim over with water
It's perfectly fair

The pavements are dealt out the dice
Every moment arrive somewhere

You can hear the hearses getting lost in lungs
Their bells stalling
And then silence comes with the plate and I
Give what I can

Feeling *It's worth it*

For I see
What my votes the mice are accomplishing
And I know I'm free

This is how I live
Up here and simply

Others do otherwise
Maybe

THE LAST ONE

Well they'd made up their minds to be everywhere because
     why not.
Everywhere was theirs because they thought so.
They with two leaves they whom the birds despise.
In the middle of stones they made up their minds.
They started to cut.

Well they cut everything because why not.
Everything was theirs because they thought so.
It fell into its shadows and they took both away.
Some to have some for burning.

Well cutting everything they came to the water.
They came to the end of the day there was one left standing.
They would cut it tomorrow they went away.
The night gathered in the last branches.
The shadow of the night gathered in the shadow on the water.
The night and the shadow put on the same head.
And it said Now.

Well in the morning they cut the last one.
Like the others the last one fell into its shadow.
It fell into its shadow on the water.
They took it away its shadow stayed on the water.

Well they shrugged they started trying to get the shadow away.
They cut right to the ground the shadow stayed whole.
They laid boards on it the shadow came out on top.
They shone lights on it the shadow got blacker and clearer.
They exploded the water the shadow rocked.
They built a huge fire on the roots.
They sent up black smoke between the shadow and the sun.
The new shadow flowed without changing the old one.

They shrugged they went away to get stones.

They came back the shadow was growing.
They started setting up stones it was growing.
They looked the other way it went on growing.
They decided they would make a stone out of it.
They took stones to the water they poured them into the shadow.
They poured them in they poured them in the stones vanished.
The shadow was not filled it went on growing.
That was one day.

The next day was just the same it went on growing.
They did all the same things it was just the same.
They decided to take its water from under it.
They took away water they took it away the water went down.
The shadow stayed where it was before.
It went on growing it grew onto the land.
They started to scrape the shadow with machines.
When it touched the machines it stayed on them.
They started to beat the shadow with sticks.
Where it touched the sticks it stayed on them.
They started to beat the shadow with hands.
Where it touched the hands it stayed on them.
That was another day.

Well the next day started about the same it went on growing.
They pushed lights into the shadow.
Where the shadow got onto them they went out.
They began to stomp on the edge it got their feet.
And when it got their feet they fell down.
It got into eyes the eyes went blind.

The ones that fell down it grew over and they vanished.
The ones that went blind and walked into it vanished.
The ones that could see and stood still
It swallowed their shadows.
Then it swallowed them too and they vanished.
Well the others ran.

The ones that were left went away to live if it would let them.
They went as far as they could.
The lucky ones with their shadows.

ALPHA

I   In all the teeth Death turned over

II And the new whistles called for the first time in the streets before daybreak

III Silence the last of the liberty ships had come up the river during the night and tied up to wait until the wharf rotted away

IV At that time the civil war between the dynasties of absence had been going on for many years

V   But during that winter the lips of the last prophets had fallen from the last trees

VI They had fallen without a sound they had not stayed in spite of the assurances proceeding from the mouths of the presidents in the money pinned thick as tobacco fish over the eyes of the saints

VII And in spite of the little votes burning at the altars in front of the empty walls

VIII And the jailers' eagle headed keys renewed in the name of freedom

IX It had been many years since the final prophet had felt the hand of the future how it had no weight and had realized that he the prophet was a ghost and had climbed the cracks in the light to take his place with the others

X   The fingers of the prophets fell but were not visible because they wore no rings

XI The feet of the prophets fell but were not visible since their goal had ceased to exist

XII The hearts of the prophets fell out of the old nests

XIII   The eyes of the prophets fell and broke like rain and a people blind as hammers hurried through them in their thin shoes

XIV   The ears of the prophets fell and after that there had been no one to hear Death saying But I keep trying to remember when I was young

BETA

I   Before daybreak in the museums the skeletons of extinct horses held up the skeletons of extinct leaves to listen

II   The light was that of the insides of quills and through it the legends of Accident the hero were marching away down roads that had not been there since the last free election

III   Out of the morning stars the blood began to run down the white sky and the crowd in tears remembered who they were and raised their hands shouting Tomorrow our flag

IV   The lips of the extinct prophets still lay on the ground here and there murmuring So much for the hair of the moon

V   But all that really remained of the prophets was their hunger which continued to fall among the people like invisible fish lines without hooks

VI   And morning the carpet bagger arrived with news of victories

VII   The lovers of flutes embraced the lovers of drums again as though they trusted them

VIII   The balloon went up that said The day is ours

GAMMA

I   It had been discovered that the bread was photographs of unidentified seas and not for everyone but it was all taken care of it was put in the banks with the dead

II   It had been discovered that the bitterness of certain rivers had no source but was caused by their looking for something through the darkness and finding

III   Something lower

IV   But it was taken care of the discovery was allowed to die of its own accord

V   And Distance with his gaunt singers sat among the citizens unnoticed and never distinctly heard

VI   He stood under the posters advertising the endless newsreels of the deposition and nobody recognized him

VII   He went into the museums and sat in the undusted replicas of what was said to have been his crown and nobody saw him

VIII   He conducted a chorus of forgiveness for his poor relations the rulers

IX   Whose blessing was as the folding and unfolding of papers

DELTA

I Came the heralds with brushes

II Came the rats dragging their leashes some time before the soldiers

III Came the cripples walking on separate seas bearing on a long scroll the bill of suffering the signatures the crosses

IV Came the bearers of doors of wood and of glass came the eyes with dead wicks came the mourners with their inventories

V Cheers cheers but it was only a rehearsal

VI Yet the spirit was there and in full daylight voices of dogs were lit on the hills nibbled coins were flung from balconies and the matches tipped with blood were brought out and kept handy

VII The pictures of dead forbears were propped up at windows to be proud

VIII The darkness began to dance in the gloves and the cry caught on We have waited enough war or no war

IX Calling for the coronation of Their Own the last of the absences

IT IS MARCH

It is March and black dust falls out of the books
Soon I will be gone
The tall spirit who lodged here has
Left already
On the avenues the colorless thread lies under
Old prices

When you look back there is always the past
Even when it has vanished
But when you look forward
With your dirty knuckles and the wingless
Bird on your shoulder
What can you write

The bitterness is still rising in the old mines
The fist is coming out of the egg
The thermometers out of the mouths of the corpses

At a certain height
The tails of the kites for a moment are
Covered with footsteps

Whatever I have to do has not yet begun

BREAD AT MIDNIGHT

The judges have chains in their sleeves
To get where they are they have
Studied many flies
They drag their voices up a long hill
Announcing It is over

Well now that it is over
I remember my homeland the mountains of chaff

And hands hands deaf as starfish fetching
The bread still frozen
To the tables

CAESAR

My shoes are almost dead
And as I wait at the doors of ice
I hear the cry go up for him Caesar Caesar

But when I look out the window I see only the flatlands
And the slow vanishing of the windmills
The centuries draining the deep fields

Yet this is still my country
The thug on duty says What would you change
He looks at his watch he lifts
Emptiness out of the vases
And holds it up to examine

So it is evening
With the rain starting to fall forever

One by one he calls night out of the teeth
And at last I take up
My duty

Wheeling the president past banks of flowers
Past the feet of empty stairs
Hoping he's dead

PIECES FOR OTHER LIVES

Encouragement meant nothing

Inside it
The miners would continue to
Crawl out of their dark bodies
Extending the darkness making
It hollow
And how could they be rightly paid

Darkness gathered on the money
It lived in the dies the miners pursued it what
Was their reward

Some might bring flowers saying Nothing can last
Some anyway
Held out their whole lives in their glass hands

Sweeter than men till past the time
Some with a pure light burned but over
Their heads even theirs
Soot wrote on the ceiling
An unknown word

Shutting your eyes from the spectacle you
Saw not darkness but
Nothing

On which doors were opening

II

All that time with nothing to do
In that granite shed
The clinic by the rainy sea

While the doctor snake turned himself on at doors
In other rooms to study
Your life a small animal dying in a bottle

Out of what could be stolen and hidden you contrived
This model of the blood
A map in lost tubing and dead joints and you
Pointed out its comical story

It begins here it swells it goes along
It comes to the man sitting talking to a stick
Which he thinks is his dog or his wife
It comes to the river unwinding the stones
It takes up a thread it comes to the tailor saying
Thank you to his needle

Over and over here is the needle

It passes through his
One seam it comes to the door which is not shown

But which anyway is standing open
And beyond it there is

Salt water in unknown quantities

III

At one stroke out of the ruin
All the watches went out and
The eyes disappeared like martins into their nests

I woke to the slamming of doors and got up naked
The old wind vanished and vanished but was still there
Everyone but the cold was gone for good

And the carol of the miners had just ended

THE MOTHS

It is cold here
In the steel grass
At the foot of the invisible statue
Made by the incurables and called
Justice

At a great distance
An audience of rubber tombstones is watching
The skulls of
The leaders
Strung on the same worm

Darkness moves up the nail

And I am returning to a night long since past
In which the rain is falling and
A crying comes from the stations
And near at hand a voice a woman's
In a jug under the wind
Is trying to sing

No one has shown her
Any statue and
The music keeps rising through her
Almost beginning and
The moths
Lie in the black grass waiting

WHENEVER I GO THERE

Whenever I go there everything is changed

The stamps on the bandages the titles
Of the professors of water

The portrait of Glare the reasons for
The white mourning

In new rocks new insects are sitting
With the lights off
And once more I remember that the beginning

Is broken

No wonder the addresses are torn

To which I make my way eating the silence of animals
Offering snow to the darkness

Today belongs to few and tomorrow to no one

WISH

The star in my
Hand is falling

All the uniforms know what's no use

May I bow to Necessity not
To her hirelings

THE WAVE

I inhabited the wake of a long wave

As we sank it continued to rush past me
I knew where it had been
The light was full of salt and the air
Was heavy with crying for where the wave had come from
And why

It had brought them
From faces that soon were nothing but rain

Over the photographs they carried with them
The white forests
Grew impenetrable but as for themselves
They felt the sand slide from
Their roots of water

The harbors with outstretched arms retreated along
Glass corridors then
Were gone then their shadows were gone then the
Corridors were gone

Envelopes came each enfolding a little chalk
I inhabited the place where they opened them

I inhabited the sound of hope walking on water
Losing its way in the
Crowd so many footfalls of snow

I inhabit the sound of their pens on boxes
Writing to the dead in
Languages
I inhabit their wrappings sending back darkness
And the sinking of their voices entering
Nowhere as the wave passes

And asking where next as it breaks

NEWS OF THE ASSASSIN

The clock strikes one one one
Through the window in a line pass
The bees whose flower is death

Why the morning smelled of honey

Already how long it is since the harvest
The dead animal fallen all the same way

On the stroke the wheels recall
That they are water
An empty window has overtaken me

After the bees comes the smell of cigars
In the lobby of darkness

APRIL

When we have gone the stone will stop singing

April April
Sinks through the sand of names

Days to come
With no stars hidden in them

You that can wait being there

You that lose nothing
Know nothing

THE GODS

If I have complained I hope I have done with it

I take no pride in circumstances but there are
Occupations
My blind neighbor has required of me
A description of darkness
And I begin I begin but

All day I keep hearing the fighting in the valley
The blows falling as rice and
With what cause
After these centuries gone and they had
Each their mourning for each of them grief
In hueless ribbons hung on walls
That fell
Their moment
Here in the future continues to find me
Till night wells up through the earth

I
Am all that became of them
Clearly all is lost

The gods are what has failed to become of us
Now it is over we do not speak

Now the moment has gone it is dark
What is man that he should be infinite
The music of a deaf planet
The one note
Continues clearly this is

The other world
These strewn rocks belong to the wind
If it could use them

THE RIVER OF BEES

In a dream I returned to the river of bees
Five orange trees by the bridge and
Beside two mills my house
Into whose courtyard a blind man followed
The goats and stood singing
Of what was older

Soon it will be fifteen years

He was old he will have fallen into his eyes

I took my eyes
A long way to the calendars
Room after room asking how shall I live

One of the ends is made of streets
One man processions carry through it
Empty bottles their
Image of hope
It was offered to me by name

Once once and once
In the same city I was born
Asking what shall I say

He will have fallen into his mouth
Men think they are better than grass

I return to his voice rising like a forkful of hay

He was old he is not real nothing is real
Nor the noise of death drawing water

We are the echo of the future

On the door it says what to do to survive
But we were not born to survive
Only to live

THE WIDOW

How easily the ripe grain
Leaves the husk
At the simple turning of the planet

There is no season
That requires us

Masters of forgetting
Threading the eyeless rocks with
A narrow light

In which ciphers wake and evil
Gets itself the face of the norm
And contrives cities

The Widow rises under our fingernails
In this sky we were born we are born

And you weep wishing you were numbers
You multiply you cannot be found
You grieve
Not that heaven does not exist but
That it exists without us

You confide
In images in things that can be
Represented which is their dimension you
Require them you say This
Is real and you do not fall down and moan

Not seeing the irony in the air

Everything that does not need you is real

The Widow does not
Hear you and your cry is numberless

This is the waking landscape
Dream after dream after dream walking away through it
Invisible invisible invisible

LOOKING EAST AT NIGHT

Death
White hand
The moths fly at in the darkness

I took you for the moon rising

Whose light then
Do you reflect

As though it came out of the roots of things
This harvest pallor in which

I have no shadow but myself

THE CHILD

Sometimes it is inconceivable that I should be the age I am
Almost always it is at a dry point in the afternoon
I cannot remember what
I am waiting for and in my astonishment I
Can hear the blood crawling over the plains
Hurrying on to arrive before dark
I try to remember my faults to make sure
One after the other but it is never
Satisfactory the list is never complete

At times night occurs to me so that I think I have been
Struck from behind I remain perfectly
Still feigning death listening for the
Assailant perhaps at last
I even sleep a little for later I have moved
I open my eyes the lanternfish have gone home in darkness
On all sides the silence is unharmed
I remember but I feel no bruise

Then there are the stories and after a while I think something
Else must connect them besides just this me
I regard myself starting the search turning
Corners in remembered metropoli
I pass skins withering in gardens that I see now
Are not familiar
And I have lost even the thread I thought I had

If I could be consistent even in destitution
The world would be revealed
While I can I try to repeat what I believe
Creatures spirits not this posture
I do not believe in knowledge as we know it
But I forget

This silence coming at intervals out of the shell of names
It must be all one person really coming at
Different hours for the same thing
If I could learn the word for yes it could teach me questions
I would see that it was itself every time and I would
Remember to say take it up like a hand
And go with it this is at last
Yourself

The child that will lead you

A DEBT

I come on the debt again this day in November

It is raining into the yellow trees
The night kept raising white birds
The fowls of darkness entering winter
But I think of you seldom
You lost nothing you need entering death

I tell you the basket has woven itself over you
If there was grief it was in pencil on a wall
At no time had I asked you for anything

What did you take from me that I still owe you

Each time it is
A blind man opening his eyes

It is a true debt it can never be paid
How have you helped me
Is it with speech you that combed out your voice till the ends bled
Is it with hearing with waking of any kind
You in the wet veil that you chose it is not with memory
Not with sight of any kind not
Yet

It is a true debt it is mine alone
It is nameless
It rises from poverty
It goes out from me into the trees
Night falls

It follows a death like a candle
But the death is not yours

THE PLASTER

How unlike you
To have left the best of your writings here
Behind the plaster where they were never to be found
These stanzas of long lines into which the Welsh words
Had been flung like planks from a rough sea
How will I

Ever know now how much was not like you
And what else was committed to paper here
On the dark burst sofa where you would later die
Its back has left a white mark on the white wall and above that
Five and a half indistinct squares of daylight
Like pages in water
Slide across the blind plaster

Into which you slipped the creased writings as into a mail slot
In a shroud

This is now the house of the rain that falls from death
The sky is moving its things in from under the trees
In silence
As it must have started to do even then
There is still a pile of dirty toys and rags
In the corner where they found the children
Rolled in sleep

Other writings
Must be dissolving in the roof
Twitching black edges in cracks of the wet fireplaces
Stuck to shelves in the filthy pantry
Never to be found
What is like you now

Who were haunted all your life by the best of you
Hiding in your death

IN AUTUMN

The extinct animals are still looking for home
Their eyes full of cotton

Now they will
Never arrive

The stars are like that

Moving on without memory
Without having been near turning elsewhere climbing
Nothing the wall

The hours their shadows

The lights are going on in the leaves nothing to do with evening

Those are cities
Where I had hoped to live

CROWS ON THE NORTH SLOPE

When the Gentle were dead these inherited their coats
Now they gather in late autumn and quarrel over the air
Demanding something for their shadows that are naked
And silent and learning

NEW MOON IN NOVEMBER

I have been watching crows and now it is dark
Together they led night into the creaking oaks
Under them I hear the dry leaves walking
That blind man
Gathering their feathers before winter
By the dim road that the wind will take
And the cold
And the note of the trumpet

DECEMBER NIGHT

The cold slope is standing in darkness
But the south of the trees is dry to the touch

The heavy limbs climb into the moonlight bearing feathers
I came to watch these
White plants older at night
The oldest
Come first to the ruins

And I hear magpies kept awake by the moon
The water flows through its
Own fingers without end

Tonight once more
I find a single prayer and it is not for men

AFTER THE SOLSTICE

Under the east cliff the spring flows into the snow

The bird tracks end like calendars

At noon white hair
Is caught in the thorns of the abandoned vineyard
Here the sky passed

The old are buried all down the slope
Except the wrists and the ancient
Message *We are with no one*

At midnight we raise their wine to tomorrow

DECEMBER AMONG THE VANISHED

The old snow gets up and moves taking its
Birds with it

The beasts hide in the knitted walls
From the winter that lipless man
Hinges echo but nothing opens

A silence before this one
Has left its broken huts facing the pastures
Through their stone roofs the snow
And the darkness walk down

In one of them I sit with a dead shepherd
And watch his lambs

GLIMPSE OF THE ICE

I am sure now
A light under the skin coming nearer
Bringing snow
Then at nightfall a moth has thawed out and is
Dripping against the glass
I wonder if death will be silent after all
Or a cry frozen in another age

THE COLD BEFORE THE MOONRISE

It is too simple to turn to the sound
Of frost stirring among its
Stars like an animal asleep
In the winter night
And say I was born far from home
If there is a place where this is the language may
It be my country

EARLY JANUARY

A year has come to us as though out of hiding
It has arrived from an unknown distance
From beyond the visions of the old
Everyone waited for it by the wrong roads
And it is hard for us now to be sure it is here
A stranger to nothing
In our hiding places

THE ROOM

I think all this is somewhere in myself
The cold room unlit before dawn
Containing a stillness such as attends death
And from a corner the sounds of a small bird trying
From time to time to fly a few beats in the dark
You would say it was dying it is immortal

DUSK IN WINTER

The sun sets in the cold without friends
Without reproaches after all it has done for us
It goes down believing in nothing
When it has gone I hear the stream running after it
It has brought its flute it is a long way

A SCALE IN MAY

Now all my teachers are dead except silence
I am trying to read what the five poplars are writing
On the void

––––––

Of all the beasts to man alone death brings justice
But I desire
To kneel in a doorway empty except for the song

––––––

Who made time provided also its fools
Strapped in watches and with ballots for their choices
Crossing the frontiers of invisible kingdoms

––––––

To succeed consider what is as though it were past
Deem yourself inevitable and take credit for it
If you find you no longer believe enlarge the temple

––––––

Through the day the nameless stars keep passing the door
That have come all that way out of death
Without questions

––––––

The walls of light shudder and an owl wakes in the heart
I cannot call upon words
The sun goes away to set elsewhere

––––––

Before nightfall colorless petals blow under the door
And the shadows
Recall their ancestors in the house beyond death

––––––

At the end of its procession through the stone
Falling
The water remembers to laugh

EVENING

I am strange here and often I am still trying
To finish something as the light is going
Occasionally as just now I think I see
Off to one side something passing at that time
Along the herded walls under the walnut trees
And I look up but it is only
Evening again the old hat without a head
How long will it be till he speaks when he passes

THE DREAM AGAIN

I take the road that bears leaves in the mountains
I grow hard to see then I vanish entirely
On the peaks it is summer

HOW WE ARE SPARED

At midsummer before dawn an orange light returns to the
    mountains
Like a great weight and the small birds cry out
And bear it up

THE DRAGONFLY

Hoeing the bean field here are the dragonfly's wings
From this spot the wheat once signalled
With lights *It is all here*
With these feet on it
My own
And the hoe in my shadow

PROVISION

All morning with dry instruments
The field repeats the sound
Of rain
From memory
And in the wall
The dead increase their invisible honey
It is August
The flocks are beginning to form
I will take with me the emptiness of my hands
What you do not have you find everywhere

THE HERDS

Climbing northward
At dusk when the horizon rose like a hand I would turn aside
Before dark I would stop by the stream falling through black ice
And once more celebrate our distance from men

As I lay among stones high in the starless night
Out of the many hoof tracks the sounds of herds
Would begin to reach me again
Above them their ancient sun skating far off

Sleeping by the glass mountain
I would watch the flocks of light grazing
And the water preparing its descent
To the first dead

THE MOURNER

On the south terraces of the glass palace
That has no bells
My hoe clacks in the bean rows
In the cool of the morning

At her hour
The mourner approaches on her way to the gate
A small old woman an aunt in the world
Without nephews or nieces
Her black straw hat shining like water
Floats back and forth climbing
Along the glass walls of the terraces
Bearing its purple wax rose

We nod as she passes slowly toward the palace
Her soft face with its tiny wattle flushed salmon
I hear her small soles receding
And remember the sound of the snow at night
Brushing the glass towers
In the time of the living

FOR THE ANNIVERSARY OF MY DEATH

Every year without knowing it I have passed the day
When the last fires will wave to me
And the silence will set out
Tireless traveller
Like the beam of a lightless star

Then I will no longer
Find myself in life as in a strange garment
Surprised at the earth
And the love of one woman
And the shamelessness of men
As today writing after three days of rain
Hearing the wren sing and the falling cease
And bowing not knowing to what

DIVINITIES

Having crowded once onto the threshold of mortality
And not been chosen
There is no freedom such as theirs
That have no beginning

The air itself is their memory
A domain they cannot inhabit
But from which they are never absent

What are you they say *that simply exist*
And the heavens and the earth bow to them
Looking up from their choices
Perishing

All day and all night
Everything that is mistaken worships them
Even the dead sing them an unending hymn

THE DRY STONE MASON

The mason is dead the gentle drunk
Master of dry walls
What he made of his years crosses the slopes without wavering
Upright but nameless
Ignorant in the new winter
Rubbed by running sheep
But the age of mortar has come to him

Bottles are waiting like fallen shrines
Under different trees in the rain
And stones drip where his hands left them
Leaning slightly inwards
His thirst is past

As he had no wife
The neighbors found where he kept his suit
A man with no family they sat with him
When he was carried through them they stood by their own dead
And they have buried him among the graves of the stones

IN THE WINTER OF MY
THIRTY-EIGHTH YEAR

It sounds unconvincing to say *When I was young*
Though I have long wondered what it would be like
To be me now
No older at all it seems from here
As far from myself as ever

Waking in fog and rain and seeing nothing
I imagine all the clocks have died in the night
Now no one is looking I could choose my age
It would be younger I suppose so I am older
It is there at hand I could take it
Except for the things I think I would do differently
They keep coming between they are what I am
They have taught me little I did not know when I was young

There is nothing wrong with my age now probably
It is how I have come to it
Like a thing I kept putting off as I did my youth

There is nothing the matter with speech
Just because it lent itself
To my uses

Of course there is nothing the matter with the stars
It is my emptiness among them
While they drift farther away in the invisible morning

WHEN YOU GO AWAY

for Dido

When you go away the wind clicks around to the north
The painters work all day but at sundown the paint falls
Showing the black walls
The clock goes back to striking the same hour
That has no place in the years

And at night wrapped in the bed of ashes
In one breath I wake
It is the time when the beards of the dead get their growth
I remember that I am falling
That I am the reason
And that my words are the garment of what I shall never be
Like the tucked sleeve of a one-armed boy

THE ASIANS DYING

When the forests have been destroyed their darkness remains
The ash the great walker follows the possessors
Forever
Nothing they will come to is real
Nor for long
Over the watercourses
Like ducks in the time of the ducks
The ghosts of the villages trail in the sky
Making a new twilight

Rain falls into the open eyes of the dead
Again again with its pointless sound
When the moon finds them they are the color of everything

The nights disappear like bruises but nothing is healed
The dead go away like bruises
The blood vanishes into the poisoned farmlands
Pain the horizon
Remains
Overhead the seasons rock
They are paper bells
Calling to nothing living

The possessors move everywhere under Death their star
Like columns of smoke they advance into the shadows
Like thin flames with no light
They with no past
And fire their only future

WHEN THE WAR IS OVER

When the war is over
We will be proud of course the air will be
Good for breathing at last
The water will have been improved the salmon
And the silence of heaven will migrate more perfectly
The dead will think the living are worth it we will know
Who we are
And we will all enlist again

PEASANT

All those years that you ate and changed
And grew under my picture
You saw nothing
It was only when I began to appear
That you said I must vanish

What could I do I thought things were real
Cruel and wise
And came and went in their names
I thought I would wait I was shrewder but you
Were dealing in something else

You were always embarrassed by what fed you
And made distances faster
Than you destroyed them
It bewitched my dreams
Like magazines I took out with the sheep
That helped to empty the hours
I tried to despise you for what you did not
Need to be able to do
If I could do it
Maybe I could have done without you

My contempt for you
You named ignorance and my admiration for you
Servility
When they were among the few things we had in common
Your trash and your poses were what I most appreciated
Just as you did

And the way you were free
Of me
But I fought in your wars
The way you could decide that things were not
And they died
The way you had reasons
Good enough for your time

When God was dying you bought him out
As you were in a position to do
Coming in the pale car through the mud and fresh dung
Unable to find the place though you had been there
Once at least before
Like the doctor
Without a moment to lose
I was somewhere
In the bargain

I was used to standing in the shade of the sky
A survivor
I had nothing you
Could use

I am taking my hands
Into the cleft wood assembled
In dry corners of abandoned barns
Beams being saved
For nothing broken doors pieces of carts
Other shadows have gone in there and
Wait
On hewn feet I follow the hopes of the owls
For a time I will

Drift down from the tool scars in a fine dust
Noticeably before rain in summer
And at the time of the first thaws
And at the sound of your frequent explosions
And when the roofs
Fall it will be a long while
Since anyone could still believe in me
Any more than if I were one of the
Immortals

It was you
That made the future
It was yours to take away
I see
Oh thousand gods
Only you are real
It is my shame that you did not
Make me
I am bringing up my children to be you

FOR A COMING EXTINCTION

Gray whale
Now that we are sending you to The End
That great god
Tell him
That we who follow you invented forgiveness
And forgive nothing

I write as though you could understand
And I could say it
One must always pretend something
Among the dying
When you have left the seas nodding on their stalks
Empty of you
Tell him that we were made
On another day

The bewilderment will diminish like an echo
Winding along your inner mountains
Unheard by us
And find its way out
Leaving behind it the future
Dead
And ours

When you will not see again
The whale calves trying the light
Consider what you will find in the black garden
And its court
The sea cows the Great Auks the gorillas
The irreplaceable hosts ranged countless
And fore-ordaining as stars
Our sacrifices

Join your word to theirs
Tell him
That it is we who are important

IN A CLEARING

The unnumbered herds flow like lichens
Along the darkness each carpet at its height
In silence
Herds without end
Without death
Nothing is before them nothing after
Among the hooves the hooves' brothers the shells
In a sea

Passing through senses
As through bright clearings surrounded with pain
Some of the animals
See souls moving in their word death
With its many tongues that no god could speak
That can describe
Nothing that cannot die

The word
Surrounds the souls
The hide they wear
Like a light in the light
And when it goes out they vanish

In the eyes of the herds there is only one light
They cherish it with the darkness it belongs to
They take their way through it nothing is
Before them and they leave it
A small place
Where dying a sun rises

AVOIDING NEWS BY THE RIVER

As the stars hide in the light before daybreak
Reed warblers hunt along the narrow stream
Trout rise to their shadows
Milky light flows through the branches
Fills with blood
Men will be waking

In an hour it will be summer
I dreamed that the heavens were eating the earth
Waking it is not so
Not the heavens
I am not ashamed of the wren's murders
Nor the badger's dinners
On which all worldly good depends
If I were not human I would not be ashamed of anything

DEATH OF A FAVORITE BIRD

What was the matter with life on my shoulder
Age that I was wing delight
That you had to thresh out your breath in the spiked rafters
To the beat of rain
I have asked this question before it knows me it comes
Back to find me through the cold dreamless summer
And the barn full of black feathers

FLY

I have been cruel to a fat pigeon
Because he would not fly
All he wanted was to live like a friendly old man

He had let himself become a wreck filthy and confiding
Wild for his food beating the cat off the garbage
Ignoring his mate perpetually snotty at the beak
Smelling waddling having to be
Carried up the ladder at night content

Fly I said throwing him into the air
But he would drop and run back expecting to be fed
I said it again and again throwing him up
As he got worse
He let himself be picked up every time
Until I found him in the dovecote dead
Of the needless efforts

So that is what I am

Pondering his eye that could not
Conceive that I was a creature to run from

I who have always believed too much in words

THE FINDING OF REASONS

Every memory is abandoned
As waves leave their shapes
The houses stand in tears as the sun rises

Even Pain
That is a god to the senses
Can be forgotten
Until he returns in the flashing garments
And the senses themselves
Are to be taken away like clothing
After a sickness

Proud of their secrets as the dead
Our uses forsake us
That have been betrayed
They follow tracks that lead before and after
And over water
The prints cross us
When they have gone we find reasons

As though to relinquish a journey
Were to arrive
As though we had not been made
Of distances that would not again be ours
As though our feet would come to us once more
Of themselves freely
To us
Their forgotten masters

To listen to the announcements you would think
The triumph
Were ours

As the string of the great kite Sapiens
Cuts our palms
Along predestined places
Leaving us
Leaving
While we find reasons

COME BACK

You came back to us in a dream and we were not here
In a light dress laughing you ran down the slope
To the door
And knocked for a long time thinking it strange

Oh come back we were watching all the time
With the delight choking us and the piled
Grief scrambling like guilt to leave us
At the sight of you
Looking well
And besides our questions our news
All of it paralyzed until you were gone

Is it the same way there

WATCHERS

The mowers begin
And after this morning the fox
Will no longer glide close to the house in full day
When a breath stirs the wheat
Leaving his sounds waiting at a distance
Under a few trees

And lie out
Watching from the nodding light the birds on the roofs
The noon sleep

Perhaps nothing
For some time will cross the new size of the stubble fields
In the light
And watch us
But the day itself coming alone
From the woods with its hunger
Today a tall man saying nothing but taking notes
Tomorrow a colorless woman standing
With her reproach and her bony children
Before rain

MY BROTHERS THE SILENT

My brothers the silent
At any hour finding
Blackness to stand in like cold stars my brothers
The invisible
What an uncharitable family
My brothers shepherds older than birth
What are you afraid of since I was born
I cannot touch the inheritance what is my age to you
I am not sure I would know what to ask for
I do not know what my hands are for
I do not know what my wars are deciding
I cannot make up my mind
I have the pitiless blood and the remote gaze of our lineage
But I will leave nothing to strangers
Look how I am attached to the ends of things
Even your sheep our sheep
When I meet them on the roads raise toward me
Their clear eyes unknowable as days
And if they see me do not recognize me do not
Believe in me

IN ONE OF THE RETREATS OF MORNING

There are still bits of night like closed eyes in the walls
And at their feet the large brotherhood of broken stones
Is still asleep
I go quietly along the edge of their garden
Looking at the few things they grow for themselves

LOOKING FOR MUSHROOMS AT SUNRISE

for Jean and Bill Arrowsmith

When it is not yet day
I am walking on centuries of dead chestnut leaves
In a place without grief
Though the oriole
Out of another life warns me
That I am awake

In the dark while the rain fell
The gold chanterelles pushed through a sleep that was not mine
Waking me
So that I came up the mountain to find them

Where they appear it seems I have been before
I recognize their haunts as though remembering
Another life

Where else am I walking even now
Looking for me

W. S. MERWIN

W. S. Merwin was born in New York City in 1927 and grew up in Union City, New Jersey, and in Scranton, Pennsylvania. From 1949 to 1951 he worked as a tutor in France, Portugal, and Majorca. After that, for several years he made the greater part of his living by translating from French, Spanish, Latin and Portuguese. Since 1954 several fellowships have been of great assistance. In addition to poetry, he has written articles, chiefly for *The Nation,* and radio scripts for the BBC. He has lived in Spain, England, France, Mexico and Hawaii, as well as New York City. His books of poetry are *A Mask for Janus* (1952), *The Dancing Bears* (1954), *Green with Beasts* (1956), *The Drunk in the Furnace* (1960), *The Moving Target* (1963), *The Lice* (1967), *The Carrier of Ladders* (1970), for which he was awarded the Pulitzer Prize, *Writings to an Unfinished Accompaniment* (1973), *The Compass Flower* (1977) and *Opening the Hand* (1983). His translations include *The Poem of the Cid* (1959), *Spanish Ballads* (1960), *The Satires of Persius* (1961), *Lazarillo de Tormes* (1962), *The Song of Roland* (1963), *Selected Translations* (1948–1968 (1968), for which he won the P.E.N. Translation Prize for 1968, *Transparence of the World,* a translation of his selection of poems by Jean Follain (1969), *Osip Mandelstam, Selected Poems* (with Clarence Brown) (1974), *Selected Translations* 1968–1978 (1979), *From the Spanish Morning* (1984) and *Four French Plays* (1984). He has also published three books of prose, *The Miner's Pale Children* (1970), *Houses and Travellers* (1977) and *Unframed Originals* (1982). In 1974 he was awarded The Fellowship of the Academy of American Poets. In 1979 he was awarded the Bollingen Prize for Poetry.